y Matters

Dollars

By Mary Hill

Children's Press®
A Division of Scholastic Inc.
New York / Toronto / London / Auckland / Sydney
Mexico City / New Delhi / Hong Kong
Danbury, Connecticut

Photo Credits: Cover © Mark Scott/Getty Images; pp. 5, 7, 9, 15, 21 by Maura B. McConnell; pp. 11, 13 © Joseph Sohm; Visions of America/Corbis; p. 17 © James Leynse/Corbis; p. 19 © Bettmann/Corbis
Contributing Editor: Shira Laskin
Book Design: Mindy Liu

Library of Congress Cataloging-in-Publication Data

Hill, Mary, 1977–
    Dollars / by Mary Hill.
    p. cm. — (Money matters)
    Includes index.
    ISBN 0-516-25057-4 (lib. bdg.) — ISBN 0-516-25170-8 (pbk.)
    1. Dollar (Coin)—Juvenile literature. I. Title.

CJ1835.H553 2005
737.4973—dc22
                                                2004007205

Contents

A **dollar** is a kind of money.

Dollars can be made of paper or **metal**.

A dollar **bill** is paper money.

It is made of **cotton**
and **linen**.

7

A dollar bill is worth one hundred **pennies**.

9

George Washington is on the front of the dollar bill.

He was the first president of the United States of America.

11

The **Great Seal of the United States** is on the back of the dollar bill.

It is made up of two pictures that stand for the United States of America.

13

There are also five, ten, twenty, fifty, and one hundred dollar bills.

15

The United States also has a dollar **coin**.

Sacagawea is on the dollar coin.

Sacagawea was a **famous Native American**.

She helped Americans who came to the West.

19

There are many different kinds of dollars.

21

New Words

bill (**bil**) a piece of paper money

coin (**koin**) a piece of metal with a picture and number on it that is used as money

cotton (**kaht**-n) the cloth made from a cotton plant

dollar (**dahl**-uhr) an amount of money equal to one hundred pennies

famous (**fay**-muhss) known by many people

Great Seal of the United States (**grayt seel uv thee yoo**-nyt-uhd **stayts**) the official seal of the United States

linen (**lin**-uhn) cloth made from the flax plant

metal (**met**-l) a hard material that comes from the ground that is used for many things, such as pots, coins, parts of cars, and jewelry

Native American (**nay**-tiv uh-**mer**-uh-kuhn) one of the original inhabitants of North, Central, or South America or a descendant of these

pennies (**pen**-eez) small metal coins that are reddish-brown in color, and are each worth one cent

Sacagawea (sak-uh-juh-**wee**-uh) a famous Native American woman who helped Americans explore the West in 1804

To Find Out More

Books
The Go-Around Dollar
by Barbara Johnston Adams
Simon & Schuster Children's Publishing

The Story of Money
by Betsy C. Maestro
HarperCollins Children's Book Group

Web Site
Money Central Station
http://www.moneyfactory.com/kids/start.html
This Web site has lots of information about money and
fun games to play.

Index

About the Author
Mary Hill is a children's book author. She has written books about many different subjects.

Reading Consultants
Kris Flynn, Coordinator, Small School District Literacy, The San Diego County Office of Education

Shelly Forys, Certified Reading Recovery Specialist, W.J. Zahnow Elementary School, Waterloo, IL

Paulette Mansell, Certified Reading Recovery Specialist, and Early Literacy Consultant, TX